LAWS & CHARTERS

Edgar,
King of the English

Translated by: D.P. Curtin

Dalcassian Publishing Company
PHILADELPHIA, PA

LAWS & CHARTERS

Copyright @ 2015 Dalcassian Publishing Company

All rights reserved. No part of this publication may be reproduced, distributed, or transmitted in any form or by any means, including photocopying, recording, or other electronic or mechanical methods, without the prior written permission of the publisher, except in the case of brief quotations embodied in critical reviews and certain other non-commercial uses permitted by copyright law. For permission request, write to Dalcassian Publishing Company at dalcassianpublishing at gmail.com

ISBN: 979-8-8692-1090-6 (Paperback)

Library of Congress Control Number:
Author: Curtin, D.P. (1985-)

Printed by Ingram Content Group, 1 Ingram Blvd, La Vergne, Tennessee

First printing edition 2015.

LAWS & CHARTERS

LAWS & CHARTERS

PAPER OF OSWADESLAU

By the bountiful mercy of the mighty God, who is King of kings and Lord of lords, I, Edgar the Basle of the English, and of all the kings of the islands of the ocean which surround Britain, and of all the nations which are included under it, emperor and lord, I thank God himself, my almighty king, who has thus enlarged my empire and he exalted above the kingdom of my fathers, who, although they had obtained the monarchy of all England, since the time of Aestelstan, who was the first of the English kings to subjugate by arms all the nations that inhabit Britain, yet none of them attempted to extend his empire beyond its borders. But the gracious divinity granted me, under the rule of the English, all the kingdoms of the islands of the Ocean, with their fiercest kings, as far as Norway, and the greatest part of Ireland, with its most noble city, Dublin, under the kingdom of the English; whom also, by the favor of God, I drove them all to submit to my command.

LAWS & CHARTERS

For this reason I, too, devoutly determined to exalt the glory and praise of Christ in my kingdom, and to enlarge his service, and through my faithful supporters, that is to say, Dunstan the archbishop, and Athelwold and Oswald the bishops (whom I chose to be my spiritual fathers and counselors) in a large part, according to arranged, completed, etc.

If, indeed, in the days of my predecessors, the English kings, the monasteries, both of monks and virgins, were destroyed and utterly rejected throughout England, which I devoted to the praise of God for the remedy of my soul, and to multiply the number of God's servants and handmaids. And with my aforesaid co-workers energetically cheering, I have already established forty-seven monasteries with monks and nuns: and if Christ has granted me life for so long, I have resolved to extend the offering of my devout God's bounty to the fiftieth number of remission (that is, the jubilee).

Wherefore now at present the monastery which the aforesaid reverend bishop Oswaldus, in the episcopal see of Wiogreceaster, enlarged in honor of the holy mother of God Mary, and having eliminated the lasciviousness and filthy lasciviousness of the clergy, he leased it to the religious servants of God, the monks with my consent and support: I myself the royal men of the monastic religion I confirm it by authority, and I strengthen and entrust it with the advice and agreement of my princes and nobles, so that there is no longer any right or right for the clerics to complain about anything therefrom; since they chose, at the risk of their own order and the expense of ecclesiastical favors, to cling to their wives rather than to serve God chastely and canonically. And therefore all that they possessed of the church, with the church itself, whether ecclesiastical or secular, both movable and immovable, I deliver and consign to the servants of God, the monks, from this day perpetually in possession of royal munificence by right, so firmly as to no princes, nor even to any succeeding bishop, it may be lawful either to withdraw anything lawful therefrom, or to penetrate, or to steal from their power, and to transfer it again to the right of the clergy, so long as the Christian faith continued in England, etc.

These things were done in the year of Dominic's incarnation 964, indictment VIII, the sixth of the reign of Edgar, king of the English, in the royal city which is named by the inhabitants [...]; on the Lord's birthday, the feast of the holy Innocents, on Wednesday.

SUBSCRIPTIONS.

I, Eadgar, basileus of the English and emperor of the kings of the nations, with the consent of both my princes and archbishops, confirm this generosity with the sign of the cross.
I, Aelfrith, the queen, agreed, and confirmed it with the sign of the cross.
I, Dunstan, archbishop of the Church of Christ in Doroburn, have consented and subscribed.
I Oscitel, Archbishop of the Church of York, have consented and subscribed.
I am Aferic, the leader.
I am Bruthnod, the leader.
I am Adrigari, the leader.

THE LAWS OF THE ECCLESIASTICAL COUNCIL OF BRANDFORD

The formulas of the acts do not occur in the council: but they are briefly thus noted in the Antiquities of the British Church, ch. 13: Meanwhile the Mercians and the Norsemen, and between the Humber and the Thames inland, take up arms against King Edwin. But the monks cautiously omit those from whom this tumult had been caused. In this tumult, Edgar, the king's brother, takes part in the kingdom. These, by many battles fought on both sides, weakened the strength of the kingdom: but Edgar at last prevailed, having convened a council of the kingdom at Brandan, annulled the acts and decrees of his brother Edwin, restored the riches which had been taken from the churches and monasteries, and recalled Dunstan from exile to his former honor, and then to the bishopric of Wigorn, unwilling , as they say, and promoted him willingly, afterwards to London, and finally, after two years had scarcely passed, to the archpriestship of Canterbury.

A privilege by which King Edgar confirms that the Church of Dorobern is the mother and mistress of the other Churches of his kingdom.

(Given in the year 959 but placed here on the occasion of the superior council.)

In the year of Dominic's incarnation 958. I, namely, Edgar, king of the English, and by divine clemency the monarch, established the ancient kings of Ethelbert and his successors, and the archbishops of Brythwald and Athelard, and the privileges of the monasteries of Kancegen, with the advice and counsel of the venerable archpontiff Dunstan, for the curse of the impious robbers, nay, more in the favor of God, for the benevolence of the just. we renew the blessing, the eternal conclusion, and strengthen it in the Lord supreme, decreeing

that the Church of Christ in Dorobernia may be the mother and mistress of the other Churches of our kingdom, and with all her people may be perpetually free everywhere, except for the expedition, the construction of bridges and forts.

A CHARTER GRANTED TO THE NEW MONASTERY OF WINCHESTER

It begins with a charter of privileges granted to the most kind prince Edgar in the new monastery of Winton, which is just called Hyda; whose rubric is thus deleted:

King Edgar issued this privilege to the new monastery and granted him great praises of the Almighty Lord and of his mother Mary.

The Almighty, the creator of the whole machine, miraculously controls all that he created with ineffable piety, who, with the eternal Word, produced some things from nothing, and some from the formless and subtle artificer propagated matter. For the angelic creature, as formless matter, having no existing things, divinely formed, shone forth with a bright face. Bad, alas! using his free will, defiant and arrogant in pride, disdaining to serve the Creator of the universe, equating himself to the Creator, drowning in the eternal barrage of fires with his accomplices, the judgment is deservedly tortured by misery. Therefore, the theme of all crime is sin.

II. Why did he create man, and what did he commit to him?

The seat of the poles having been emptied, and the soul [strongly, for HARD.] the seat of the poles, and the filthiness of the swollen pride eliminated, the Supreme Judge of all goodness did not suffer the bright seats of the heavens to be numb without a worshiper, formed from the formless matter of different species of things, at last he fashioned man, seasoned from mud, with the breath of life to himself similitude, to which he subjected the entire surface of the entire cosmos, he subjected himself and his posterity to himself, inasmuch as his execution posterity would supplement the number of the angels, pushed down from the seats of the heavens with swelling pride.

III. How he was in paradise without guilt.

He who was ensconced in the delights of paradisiacal pleasure suffered the expense of nothing but had the opportunity to supply him with the whole world at his wish. For Tousius, enjoying the abundance of goodness, had no instinctive resistance to him. By loving Altithron and devoutly obeying the creature, all things were subjugated. He enjoyed the joyous dance of the Creator, and the company of angels used him enthusiastically. He was not weakened by physical infirmity, nor was he afflicted by anxiety of mind. He was not carried away by a light typhoon of pride, but joining himself to his author, humbled himself wonderfully. Glory did not torment him, swollen with nothing, but the memory of the devotee of the Creator magnified him. It was not envy that tormented him at the stranger's departure, but charity constantly rejoiced in its embrace. He was not tormented by wrath, but by the calmness of charity the most patient was relieved. He was not cast down by sadness and sorrow, but he flourished powerfully in the hope of spiritual joy. He was not overly motivated by avarice, but he was very generous with the desire to be generous. The mass did not take pleasure in food unlawfully, but contented with frugality he used lawful food. It was not lust that incited him, which was evil, but continence, which was appropriate, constrained him to rewards; A polycrat of all virtues, lacking in all adversity, flourishing in all prosperity, he rightly flourished as an ingenuous man.

IV. How he trusted to ascend to heaven without death, and the jealous devil prevented him from ascending.

He who, with his progeny numbered, accompanied by the whole lineage of the proud angels, having tasted the fruit of the forbidden tree at the end of the bath, Macrobius trusted to ascend the ethereal platform of eternal bliss reigning in trinity with the Lord. Zabulus, therefore, perceiving this, the envious man, greatly moved by envy, had begun to devise cunning tricks, which he would deceive by scheming, lest he should ascend to such a glory of the deity; for nothing, perhaps leading, granted, by praising the illicit too much, he drove away a very frail woman. She, not at all satisfied with her own loss, destroyed her husband, who had lived in a womanly manner, beguiled by flattering persuasions;

V. How in this misery they are cast down, deprived of all their virtues, and finally by the cataclysm of [...]

Both are finally deprived of the aforesaid gifts, deprived of the fruits of paradise, and thrown into the misery of the present life, despising the founder, pursued by all creatures. Life ceased, death entered. As the group of virtues receded, an accumulation of vices succeeded. After the descendants of the grandsons, there succeeded a collegium (collection) of accumulated crimes: all of them were brought down by the cataclysm with their crimes, and finally, eight of each sex being reserved, they fail by melting. Abounding in vices, the Founder lamented that he had made himself a man. Finally, as he had promised, he succored the merciful mortals.

VI. How Christ, born by his own passion, redeemed us, and caused us to ascend into the heavens.

The morning star shone, which with its rays would dispel the darkness of the world. Fausta shines on Mary, in whose virginal womb Christ was born indescribably, the most merciful mediator of the darkness of sins. Christ lived full of virtues. Judea was enraged, filled with great resentment. Taking on flesh, he was willing to suffer for us; which, with his permission, the unfortunate man boldly completed Judaea. For the lost tree, climbing the tree, redeems the human race. For the devil mockingly insulted the nations of all men, possessing the law as a transgressor of the commandment, punishing him with perpetual death. But the blood of the dead divided the avenger with the trophy of the cross. He took the prey from the mouth of the perfidious lion, and, riding on the ether, associated himself with the groups of angels above, so that with him, enjoying a common company, filled with the goodness of the transparent, filled with the abundance of all virtues, experienced in sin, deprived of all contamination, and reigning without end, rejoicing in the restored bodies after the day of judgment. Having promised this special glory without doubt to those who believe, who follow the faith of the Trinity and the true unity by good works, and to those who do not believe he threatens eternal punishment by perpetual burnings, he most justly promises.

VII. Of the benevolent meditation of the king.

From this I, Edgar, the basileus of all Albion, by the divine favor, began to ponder greatly what works I should pursue in the pursuit of such glory, that, having attained such glory, I should enjoy being crowned with the company of Christ and his saints placed in heaven, and should be enriched by such misery of hell. Urging indeed the Lord's clemency, he met his mind that he himself should cease from all crimes, and persisting in good works, becoming the form of the flock, so long as we should profit those who live under the government of our government. Therefore, inviting some to rewards by persuasions, compelling others to glory by terrors, I built up good things, and destroyed evils, as I could by doing them to the Lord. For I remember what was written by Jeremiah the prophet: Behold, I have appointed thee over nations and over kingdoms, to pull up, and to destroy, and to scatter, and to scatter, and to build, and to plant (Jeremiah 1). Exhorted, therefore, by such teachers, to whom the Lord kindly admonished us through the prophet, doing in favor of Christ on earth what he justly did in the heavens, that is to say, rooting out the impurity of the Lord's culture of crimes, I diligently sowed the seeds of virtue.

VIII. By this means, eliminating the clergy, he placed the monks.

Fearing lest I should incur eternal misery, if, having obtained power, I did not do what he, who works all that he wills in heaven and on earth, made known by his examples to the just examiner, I removed the vices of the vicious canons from the different cenobies of our government, vicar of Christ; that they could not profit me by any intercessions, but rather, as the blessed Gregory says, they should provoke the vengeance of the just Judges, who, contaminated by vicarious vicarious vices, did not do what God willed by commanding, but rebelled against all that He did not want. An avid inquisitor, noting that the monks were grateful to the Lord, who would intercede for us unceasingly, I cheerfully placed the devotees of our right monasteries.

IX. Which, by the grace of the Holy Spirit, appointed an abbot and monks in a new monastery.

On this account therefore, touched by the breath of the Holy Spirit, cleansing the place of the Lord in the church of Winton, the barracks of the new monastery dedicated to our savior and to his mother the ever-virgin Mary, and to all the apostles, together with the other saints, I restored. Knowing that it is written: Those who agree and do are equally constrained by the punishment of rebellion, meeting the will of the Almighty. Not enduring to usurp the possession of the Lord, I repelled the lascivious clerics, and the true worshipers of God officiating at the monastic level, who would diligently intercede for the excesses of ours and those resting there, so that the state of our government might be strengthened by their intercessions. I exclaim in support of this, that what I have done in his own, this he may do in mine, that is to say, by casting down our adversaries, by exalting our friends, as I have justified by depressing the enemies of the holy Church of God, by beatifying his friends, the monks.

X. Concerning the anathema of those who lie in wait for the monks.

But if, on any occasion, at the instigation of the devil, it should happen that, in the pride of proud arrogance, deposed canons, they wished to cast down a flock of monks, whom I, as a venerable shepherd, had placed in the possession of God, by ambush, let it be done against them and against all those who, blinded by any function, have paid them aid, that It is about proud angels, and about the progenitor of the devil deceived by fraud, that is to say, the borders and cast out from the lofty seats of heaven, together with those who despised the servant of the Lord, thrust out by burning barathers, shall be tortured by the yoke of misery. And those who were torn from thence should not boast that they had escaped the torments, but with Judas, the betrayer of Christ, and his accomplices, glued to the Acheron, shrieking with cold, consumed by fever, deprived of joy, anxious with sorrow, bound by fiery chains, shaken by the fear of punishments, confused by the memory of crimes, isolated from the memory of all goodness, eternally sad they must be punished by torture.

XI. Also about the anathema of those who lie in wait.

But whoever presumptuously presuming to eliminate the aforesaid new monks of the church of Winton, or any of the same order living under our rule, purges the monasteries of the filth of vices, which Jesus Christ our Lord, the vanquished demon, has acquired, let him be anathema. and by the same curse with which Cain, the parricide, who, stirring up envy, his brother Abel, bruised and killed the flagellum, was brought to be bound without end; and persevering continually in the persecution of God, in this life he acquires no honor of dignity, nor in the future will he ever persevere without misery, but with Ananias and Sapphira together with the Styx he embraces the tormenting one with a torrent.

XII. On the blessing of the visiting monks.

Whoever wishes to enrich the pre-titled monks by enriching them with any good, the omnipotent Creator will graciously enrich them and their descendants with the abundance of prosperity here and in the world to come. Having written their names decently in the book of life, may they have a portion with Christ in the dwellings of heaven, who have honored his monks, whom he has gathered in our times, either by word or deed, in the pursuit of holiness.

XIII The nature and quality of the monks are preserved in this monastery.

Therefore, regular monks, not secular, in the aforesaid, with Christ, living in the monastery, obeying the moral rules, venerating the spiritual Fathers, imitating the examples of the holy Fathers, doing nothing except what the common rule of the monastery, or the norm of the elders has shown.

Therefore, removed from worldly pomp, let them guard the chastity of body and soul with all their efforts. Strong in the pursuit of humility, and diminishing the body by the vigor of thrift, let them constrain the zeal of the mind. The guests of the citizens within the city should be shamed by a perpetual ban. Dwelling in the city, in the refectory displaying pompous and lascivious worldly delights as melancholy, they use lawful charity for food; but not at all outside the refectory, unless the sick were lying in the house of the sick, eating what was lawfully ordered. Guests of the sacred and highest order, if reason demanded, and pilgrims of order, coming from a long distance from the world, shall be most cautiously invited to the abbot's table in the refectory; the laity should be treated with the humanity that befits hospitality. According to the decrees of the Fathers, none of the monks should have permission to eat or drink with them; but let them not be brought into the refectory for eating or drinking, let the poor, like Christ, be received with dancing by the great heart.

XIV. On the election of the abbot.

Most diligently learned in the study of the divine Scriptures, constantly engaged in the frequency of prayer, most joyful in the embrace of charity, most ready in the exercise of faith, most sincere in the progress of hope, fixed in harmony in peace, and adorned with the flower of all virtues, to the end, having begun the beginning of so much goodness, helping Christ, leading them, may they enjoy the same glorious freedom , which the blessed patron Benedict instituted for all those subject to the precept of the rule, that is to say, that after the death of the abbot the ruler at that time, the abbot. [...] order the assembly, whom all the concordance of the assembly, whether a part however small of the assembly, has chosen for a more wholesome plan.

XV. How should the king defend the abbot and the venerable monks?

The kings, therefore, whoever may be our successors, should not impose any foreign person exercising the right of tyranny over the monks, lest God, by condemning them, may dethrone them from the kingdom and their lives. But let them accept the vicar chosen by Christ's brothers with dignity, and come and enrich him with the fire of charity; Help, inasmuch as it is needed, they diligently invest in the love of Christ. For with mutual support, and in no way contradicting the precepts of the rule, let them defend the Lord's flock, not hired servants, but faithful shepherds, free from the snares of wolves, and fearless.

XVI. How can the abbot and the monks deliver the king from the temptation of the demons?

But the abbot, girded with spiritual weapons, walled from side to side with the wedge of monks, drenched with the dew of heavenly charisms, conquering the air of the devils, conquering the wiles of the demons, the king and all the clergy of his government, helping Christ, with whose power they fight, from the rabid persecution of invisible enemies, skillfully defending with the swords of the spirit, with the subtle shield of faith protecting him with protection, fighting with a strong man in triumph, let the soldier escape undaunted.

XVII. How shall the king protect the abbot and the monks from the persecution of men?

In the same way, the earthly king, strengthening the heavenly camp of the king with the strongest fortifications, conquering his adversaries with visible worldly weapons, and throwing down the rage of the enemies by annihilating them, may his Founder's pastures and flock be protected by an impregnable guard, so far as he attains to the bravery of life, he may enjoy eternal dancing with good things, which even the human eye could not in any way see , and the things which God has prepared for those who care about him do not ever ascend into the heart of man.

XVIII. On the freedom of monastic property.

Let the fields of the aforesaid monasteries, all the possessions of the monks, whether large or small, internal or external, urban or suburban, farms, fields, meadows, pastures, woods, mills, streams, be enriched with eternal freedom in the name of Christ and his Mother.

XIX. That no layman unlawfully usurps the property of a monastery.

Let no secular man presumptuously exercise the right of tyranny in Christ's culture; will not diminish, inciting the devil, that by the instinct of the Holy Spirit both by me and by my predecessors, as well as by Catholic men of both sexes, liberality has been freely granted.

XX. Of the blessing of those who grow.

May the Maker of all things grant the calm course of the present life, the longevity of the present time, the future reward of eternal bliss, the sufficient abundance of food, the endless increase of prosperity, the abundant support of all virtues.

XXI. Of the curse of those who diminish.

Let perpetual misery possess the inferior; abiding in the persecution of the Lord, he incurs offense against his Mother and all the saints; let the adversity of the present life always happen to him; no good fortune befalls them; all his treasures should be plundered by the enemy standing by; but in the future, the eternals will condemn the most wretched and tormented child placed on the left side, if he does not make amends with a suitable satisfaction for what he has brought down by usurping the censure of the Lord.

XXII. They should obey these secular methods, and that no liability should be able to diminish this privilege of the Lord.

For three reasons only, they obeyed the secular orders, that is, the expedition, the construction of a bridge, or a fort; at other times the eternally rich may glory in freedom. If, inciting a demon, seduced, or an abbot, or any of the brothers frailly, contracted what is absent, the guilt of what is pious is abolished, by the cleansing justice according to the precept of the rule, and the freedom of the aforesaid munificence, offered to Altitron through our humility, remains an inviolable, eternal freedom for the use of the monks gratuitously. joyous, because God, who possesses this generous gift of privilege, the place with the whole family of monks, and all the rights subject to the sacred convent, has never committed a crime, and will never commit it at any time. Therefore, let the aforesaid eternal liberty be, because God is the eternal possessor of liberty.

XXIII. How often and why in the circle of the year is this privilege bequeathed to the brethren.

In the nine hundred and sixty-sixth year of Dominic's incarnation, the signature of this privilege was written, with the consent of these witnesses, whose names are drawn up in order below.

SUBSCRIPTIONS.

I, Edgar, by divine grace, Basil of the English, bestowing this gift of privilege on our Redeemer, and in his most holy place, the first of all kings, establishing a college of monks there, confirmed it by impressing with my own hand the sign of the Haggian cross.
I, Dunstan, archbishop of the Church of Doroburn, respecting the generous gift of the benevolent king, strengthened it with the sign of the cross.
I, Eadmund, legitimate son of the aforesaid, put the seal of the cross, in the blooming age of a child, with my own hand.
I, Edward, begotten by the same king, consolidated the aforesaid generosity of my father with the sign of the cross.
I, Aelfthryth, the legitimate consort of the aforesaid king, appointing the monks by my delegation to the same place as the king nodding, stamped the cross.
I, Eadgifa, grandfather of the aforesaid king, consolidated this excellent work

with the thaumat of the cross.
I, Oscytyl, archbishop of the Church of York, confirmed.
I, Athelwold, bishop of the church of Winchester, commending to him the benevolence of the most glorious king, my high abbot for his modesty, and the pupils whom I had educated, I blessed him with the seal of the cross.
I, Aelfstan, the pontiff of the Church of London, consolidated.
I confirmed Osulf, the bishop.
I have sent Oswold, the bishop.
I confirmed Bysentelm, the bishop.
Ealefstan, the bishop, I consolidated.
I confirmed Eadelm, the bishop.
I, Athulf, the bishop, consigned
I confirmed Urynryge, the bishop.
Aercwig, the abbot, I consolidated.
I have entrusted Osgar, the abbot.
I, Orobyrihe, abbot.
I am Aelfstan, the abbot.
I, Adelgar, the first abbot ordained in this place.
I am Osdgar, the leader.
I am Aethelstan, the chief.
I am Athelwine, chief.
I, Aethelweard, m.
I Elfweard, m.
I, Wulrtan, m.

All those who appear to have been registered by name to this privilege by the king's order, we implore, with the support of our posterity, that they may in no way violate the pledge of our hands established by the cross of Christ, and make it null and void; if he presumes to violate any of his successors with the audacity of humility, deprived of the participation of the body and blood of Jesus Christ, condemned to perpetual perdition, let him be anathema, unless he has repented with divine propitiatory respect to earthly satisfaction.

LAWS & CHARTERS

ANOTHER LETTER OF KING EDGAR, in which he declares that there had never been any monks in this convent of Winton, before those whom he himself had already introduced from the monastery of Abingion.

At the consent of Altithron, the ruler of the whole of Albion, having obtained a triune government, I did not forget that, on this account, a relapse would be granted, so that I might gain eternally by them; wherefore I, Edgar, a native of all Britain, having certain villages, as they are named, Dunkiton, five furlongs of land, and the church of Sueyse, with twenty-eight furlongs of land, and the church of Titlescumbe, with ten furlongs of land, and a certain portion of the countryside, namely, two cottages of land, instead of who is called by the famous name Wynterburne, I give and grant in pure and perpetual alms to the new church of Winton, dedicated to B. Peter, the prince of the apostles, as well as to St. Edotius, whose relics there shine with miracles, with all utensils, that is to say, meadows, pastures, streams, be eternally endowed by a clear inheritance, so that the canons who continued to be incorrigible were expelled from the said church, the monks of Abundonia were substituted instead. And let the aforesaid towns, lands, mansions, lands, streams, be free for ever from the yoke of all earthly servitude, with the exception of three, that is to say, approved by the expedition, the bridge, or the restoration of the castle. But if anyone wishes to transfer this donation of ours to something else than we have decided, the private association of the holy Church of God, shall be punished by eternal barathri burnings in sorrowful times with Judas, the betrayer of Christ, and his accomplices, if he does not make suitable satisfaction for the violation of the decree against us.

ECCLESIASTICAL LAWS

Titles of chapters.
I. On the immunity of the Church, and the debts to be paid to it.
II. Of the ecclesiastical census, or of the firstfruits of the seed.
III. Of tithes.
IV. He put a penny in each house.
V. Of feast days and fasting.

THE LAWS OF KING EDGAR
The laws which King Edgar, in a crowded senate, sanctioned for the glory of God, the ornament of the royal majesty, and the benefit of the republic:

1. First, the church of God has all its rights and immunities; each tithe of the primary (to which he was subject) church, as indeed he himself is surrounded by plows, given, whether it was in the estates of the thanes proper, or in the lands of the vicars.

II. Now, if he had a temple in the land possessed by the writing, around which a place of burial had been designated, be wholehearted to contribute one third of his tithes to it. If no burial place had been designated around the temple, the priest who owns the land was given nine parts of the remains as he saw fit. And indeed from all the land of the first-fruits, the very first-fruits of the seeds, the primary hanger of the church.

III. Every tithe of the offspring shall be paid before Pentecost; indeed, the tithe of the fruits of the earth is due before the Equinox; and the very first fruits of the seeds were returned under the feast of the god Martin. If anyone does not pay, the penalties are given, as is given in the judicial book. And if anyone refuses to pay the tithes, to whom we have stated the manner, the royal presbyter, the bishop of that place, and the priest shall meet, and with him, whether or not he wills, the tenth part of the church to whom it is due, the ninth part of the rest shall be returned to him. As for the remaining eight parts, the lord has four, the bishop four; which is done, whether he be the minister of the king, or the thane of any other.

IV. A denarius was placed in each house, and it was returned before the feast of the god Peter. He who then did not pay, took that denarius and thirty others besides to Rome, and returning home with the sure testimony of letters, confirmed that he had brought it, and finally paid the king one hundred and twenty shillings. If anyone does not give a second time, let him carry that denarius and three denarii in addition to Rome, and the king, after he has returned, will depend on two hundred solidi. If he transgresses a third time, he shall be stripped of all his possessions.

V. On the Sabbath day from Saturday itself at three o'clock in the afternoon until the day of the lunar day I keep the festival; who did not celebrate, the punishments described in the judicial book were suspended. And the rest of the days are exactly as they have been announced by the priest, the official of the festival. Institutes even the most religiously observant of fasting.

THE EARLY VERSION OF KING EDGAR'S ECCLESIASTICAL LAW.

I. On paying the debts of the Church.
II. Of the churches where the cemetery is.
III. Of the terms of decimation.
IV. About the unwillingness to give tithes.
V. Concerning those who do not pay St. Peter's penny.
6. Of solemnities and terms to be observed.

This is the institution which King Edgar, by the counsel of his wise men, instituted for the glory of God, and for his own royal dignity, and for the benefit of his nation.

1. The first thing is that the churches of God should be worthy of their right, and that every tithe should be returned to the mother church to which the parish adjoins from the land of the Thais and peasants, as it goes through the plough.

II. If there be any one of the Thais who has a church for his fee where there is a cemetery, he shall give him a third part of his tithe. If there is no court there, let him give from his nine parts to the presbyter what he wants, and also all the circumcised to the mother church from every free house.

III. And let all the tithe of the youth be returned at Pentecost, and of the crops of the land at the Equinox, and all the circumcision at the feast of St. Martin, by full forfeiture as the book of justice says.

IV. If anyone refuses to pay the tithe, as we have said, the priest in charge of the king and the bishop is present [f. and the bishop, and the priest, etc.] of that church, and he shall return his tithe to the church to which it belongs, and they shall release the ninth part to him who withheld his tithe, and the eight parts shall be divided into two, half to the lord, half to the bishop, let him be the king's man, let him be the man of the Thain.

LAWS & CHARTERS

V. And every heordpen shall pay back at the feast of St. Peter: and whoever does not pay at that term, let him bring it to Rome, and also thirty denarii, and bring thence the meaning of what he paid there so much. And when he returns home, he will buy one hundred and twenty shillings. And if he refuses to pay again, let him bring it to Rome, and make the same amends. And when he returns, he will redeem one hundred and twenty shillings to the king. For the third time, if he still does not repay, he shall lose all that he has.

6. And the solemnity of Sunday shall be preserved from the morning of the ninth day of Saturday until the light of the day of Monday, the superstition which the book of judgments says and teaches. And another festival, as will be announced by the priest. And every prescribed fast shall be observed with all devotion.

ADDRESS TO DUNSTAN, OSWALD, AND ETHELWALD

Since the Lord has magnified his mercy to us, it is worthy, O most reverend fathers, that we should respond to his innumerable favors with worthy works. For we do not possess the earth by our sword, and it was not our arm that saved us, but his right hand and his holy arm, because he was pleased with us. It is just, therefore, that we should subject ourselves and our souls to him who has put all things under our feet, and that those whom he has subjected to us should be subject to his laws, so that we should not work lazily. And indeed, it is my interest to treat the laity with the right of equity, to make just judgment between a man and his neighbor, to punish blasphemers, to suppress rebels, to rescue the helpless from the hand of his mighty, the needy and the poor from those who plundered him. But it is also my concern, to provide for the ministers of the churches, the flocks of monks, the choirs of virgins, and their necessities, and to consult them for safety, rest, or peace. The examination of the character of all of them looks to us [f., to you], if they have lived continuously, if they have behaved honestly towards those who are abroad; if they are concerned with divine duties, if they are diligent in teaching the people, if they are sober in their diet, if they are temperate in their behavior, if they are discreet in their judgments. I speak of your peace, reverend Fathers, if you had attended to this skillful scrutiny, so horrible and abominable things would not have reached our ears from the clergy.

I am silent that the crown is not open to them, nor is the haircut suitable; but lasciviousness in dress, insolence in gesture, vulgarity in speech, betray the insanity of the inner man. Moreover, in the divine offices, what is negligence, when they hardly deign to attend the sacred vigils, when they seem to gather at the solemn solemnities of the masses to play, to smile rather than to sing. I will say that the good mourn, the bad laugh; I will tell with sorrow (and if it can be said) how they flow in revelries, in drunkenness, in beds, and indecency, so that already the houses of the clergy are thought to be the dens of harlots, the conciliators of actors. There is gambling, there dancing and singing; there until the middle of the night a protracted vigil in clamor and horror. Thus, the patrimony of kings, the alms of the poor, nay, what is more, the price of that precious blood is spent. For this, then, did our fathers exhaust their treasures? For this the king's treasury, after deducting many rents, was distributed? for this the churches of Christ contributed the fields and possessions of the royal bounties, so that the harlots were adorned with the pleasures of the clerics, luxurious banquets were prepared, dogs and birds, and such amusements were provided? This the soldiers shout, the people murmur, the mimes sing and dance, and you neglect, you spare, you hide! Where was the sword of Levi and the zeal of Simeon, who, taking advantage of Jacob's daughter as a prostitute, cut off the Sichemites (having the image of those who defame the Church of Christ by their filthy deeds) even the circumcised? Where is the spirit of Moses, who spared not even the householders of his own blood who worshiped the calf's head? Where is the dagger of Phineus the priest, who, stabbing the adulterer with the Midianite, appeased the angry God with this holy rivalry? Where is the spirit of Peter, whose power destroys covetousness, condemned to the Simonian heresy?

Rival, O priests, rival the ways of the Lord, and the judgments of our God. The time to rise up against those who destroyed the throne of God. I, Constantine, you, Peter, have a sword in your hands. Let us join hands, let us join sword with sword, that the lepers may be cast out of the camp, that the sanctuary of the Lord may be cleansed, and that the sons of Levi may minister in the temple, who said to his father and mother: I do not know you, and to his brothers: I do not know you. Act, I pray thee, diligently, that he may not repent that we have done what we have done, that we have given what we have given; if we see it consumed not in the obedience of God, but in the luxury of the worst, with unpunished liberty. Let the remains of the saints move you, in which they insult; venerable altars, before which they go mad. May you be moved by the wonderful devotion of our ancestors, whose alms are abused by clerical vexation. My great-grandfather Edward, as you know, tithed all his land to churches and monasteries. Aluredus, my ancestor of holy memory, thought that in order to enrich the church, he spared not the treasury, nor the expenses, nor the rents. My grandfather, the elder Edward did not hide your paternity as much as he contributed to the churches. My father and brother, with the gifts of which Christ's altars have been heaped up, it is fitting that they should remember you.

O Father of Fathers, Dunstan, I beseech you to behold the eyes of my Father radiating upon you from that bright spot of heaven. Hear his plaintive voices resounding with a kind of piety in your ears: You, Father Dunstan, you gave me sound advice about building monasteries, about building churches: you were my helper and co-operator in everything: you were like a shepherd, a father, and a bishop of my soul I chose the guardian of mine, of my manners. When did I not appear to you? Which stores have you ever preferred in your designs? What possessions did I not despise in commanding you? If you thought of giving something to the poor, I was available. If you judged what should be contributed to the churches, I did not postpone it. If you complained that something was lacking in monks or clerics, I supplied it. You said that almsgiving is eternal, and there is no other more fruitful than that which is given to monasteries and churches, by which the servants of God are supported, and what is left is given to the poor. O precious alms, and worth the price of the soul! O salutary remedy for our sins! that from the Sibyl's bosom the skin of the stranger's wall stinks, that adorns her ears, that she arranges her fingers, that she binds her delicate body in a byss and purple. Behold, Father, the fruits of my alms, and the effects of your permission.

What will you answer to this complaint? I know, I know: When you saw a thief, you did not run with him, nor did you cast your lot with adulterers. You pleaded, begged and rebuked. Words are contemptible, you must come to blows, and you will not lack royal power. You have here with you the venerable Father Ethelwald, bishop of Winton; you have the venerable Prince Oswald of Worcester; I entrust this task to you, so that, both by episcopal censure and by royal authority, those living in disgrace may be expelled from the churches, and those living in order may be brought in.

THE MALMESBURY PAPER

I, Edgar, the ruler of all Albion, as well as of the surrounding kings of the sea or islands, so much so that under the subjection of none of my progenitors, with the generous grace of God at hand, I was exalted, what would be the most important gift of my empire to the King of kings, mindful of so great an honor, I often negotiated more skillfully. Therefore, the pious supporter of my watchful devotion suddenly insinuated divine piety to restore the holy monasteries in my kingdom, which had been visibly torn down with mossy splinters and expensive boards, held to the rafters, so (what is greater) that they had been completely neglected within by the service of God. Idiots, that is to say, expelled clerics, subject to no regular religious discipline, in many places of the holier order, that is, of monastic habit, prefects of shepherds, presenting to them the expense of rich fiscal functions for the restoration of the dilapidated temples. One of whom, named Eluricus, a most famous ecclesiastical man, I made guardian of the convent, which the English call Maldemelsburh by the name of Maldemelsburh. To whom, for the comfort of my soul, for the sake of our Savior, and of his Θεότοκου of the ever-virgin Mary, as well as of the apostles Peter and Paul, and Aldelmia, the prefects of the alms, I restored the honor, a piece of land, and in particular the land with meadows and woods, with munificent liberality. This, having been accommodated by the aforesaid clerics, was unjustly possessed by the contentious Edolnotus: but, having heard his superstitious and subtle discussion by my wise men, and having been convicted of his false contention by the same men present to me, it was restored by me to monastic use, in the ninety and seventy-fourth year of the incarnation of Dominic, in the tenth year of my reign fourthly, in the first instance of royal conversation. This Malmesbury.

SUBSCRIPTIONS.

I, Edgar, basileus of all Albion and neighboring kings, have confirmed this signature with the sign of the holy cross.

I, Dunstan, archbishop of Doroburn, confirmed this royal gift with the trophy of the Hague's cross.

LAWS & CHARTERS

I, Oswald, Archbishop of York, signed.
I, Athelwold, bishop of Winchester, consigned.
I, Lefwinus, bishop of Dorcas, agreed.
I, Alstanus, bishop of London, of the year.
I, Turketulus, abbot of Croyland, undersigned.
I, Athelgarus, abbot of the new monastery of Winchester, approved.
I applauded, Adolphus, abbot of Burgh.
I, the leader of Alferus.
I, Athelwin the leader, stood by.
I, Captain Brithold.
And others.

LATIN TEXT

Charta de Oswadeslau

Altitonantis Dei largiflua clementia, qui est Rex regum et Dominus dominantium, ego Edgarus Anglorum basileus, omniumque regum insularum Oceani quae Britanniam circumjacent, cunctarumque nationum quae infra eam includuntur, imperator et dominus, gratias ago ipsi Deo omnipotenti regi meo, qui meum imperium sic ampliavit et exaltavit super regnum patrum meorum, qui licet monarchiam totius Angliae adepti sint, a tempore Aestelstani, qui primus regum Anglorum omnes nationes quae Britanniam incolunt sibi armis subegit, nullus tamen eorum ultra ejus fines imperium suum dilatare aggressus est. Mihi autem concessit propitia divinitas, cum Anglorum imperio omnia regna insularum Oceani cum suis ferocissimis regibus usque Norvegiam, maximam partem Hiberniae, cum sua nobilissima civitate Dublina, Anglorum regno subjugare; quos etiam omnes meis imperiis colla subdere, Dei favente gratia, coegi.

Quapropter et ego Christi gloriam et laudem in regno meo exaltare, et ejus servitium amplificare, devotus disposui, et per meos fideles fautores, Dunstanum videlicet archiepiscopum, et Athelwoldum ac Oswaldum episcopos (quos mihi Patres spirituales et consiliatores elegi) magna ex parte, secundum quod disposui, perfeci, etc.

Si quidem temporibus antecessorum meorum regum Anglorum, monasteria, tam monachorum quam virginum, destructa, penitus rejecta in tota Anglia erant, quae ego ad Dei laudem pro remedio animae meae reparare, et servorum et ancillarum Dei numerum multiplicare devovi. Et ipsis supradictis meis cooperatoribus strenue annitentibus, jam quadraginta et septem monasteria cum monachis et sanctimonialibus constitui: et si Christus vitam mihi tandiu concesserit, usque ad quinquagesimum remissionis numerum (id est jubilaei), meae devotae Dei munificentiae oblationem protendere decrevi.

Unde nunc in praesenti monasterium, quod praedictus reverendus episcopus Oswaldus, in sede episcopali Wiogreceastere, in honore sanctae Dei genitricis Mariae amplificavit, et eliminatis clericorum naeniis et spurcis lasciviis, religiosis

Dei servis monachis meo consensu et favore confultus locavit: ego ipsis monasticae religionis viris regali auctoritate confirmo, et consilio et astipulatione principum et optimatum meorum corroboro et consigno, ita ut jam amplius non sit fas neque jus clericis reclamandi quidquam inde; quippe qui magis elegerunt, cum sui ordinis periculo et ecclesiastici beneficii dispendio, suis uxoribus adhaerere quam Deo caste et canonice servire. Et ideo cuncta quae illi de ecclesia possederunt, cum ipsa ecclesia, sive ecclesiastica, sive saecularia, tam mobilia quam immobilia, ipsis Dei servis monachis ab hac die perpetualiter regiae munificentiae jure deinceps possidenda trado et consigno, ita firmiter, ut nulli principum, nec etiam ulli episcopo succedenti, fas sit aut licitum quidquam inde subtrahere, aut pervadere, aut ab eorum potestate subripere, et in clericorum jus iterum traducere, quandiu fides Christiana in Anglia perduravit, etc.

Facta sunt haec anno Dominicae incarnationis 964, indictione VIII, regni vero Edgari Anglorum regis sexto, in regia urbe quae ab incolis [...] nominatur; in natali Domini, festivitate sanctorum Innocentium, feria quarta.

SUBSCRIPTIONES.

Ego Eadgar, basileus Anglorum et imperator regum gentium, cum consensu et principum et archiepiscoporum meorum, hanc munificentiam signo crucis corroboro.
Ego Aelfrith, regina consensi, et signo crucis confirmavi.
Ego Dunstan, archiepiscopus Dorobernensis Ecclesiae Christi, consensi et subscripsi.
Ego Oscitel, archiepiscopus Eboracensis Ecclesiae, consensi et subscripsi.
Ego Aferic, dux.
Ego Bruthnod, dux.
Ego Adrigari, dux.

Leges ecclesiasticae concilii Brandafordiae

Non occurrunt in concilio actorum formulae: breviter autem sic notantur in antiquitatibus Britannicae Ecclesiae, cap. 13: Interea Mercii et Norrenses, ac inter Humbrum et Thamesim mediterranei, in regem Edwinum arma capiunt.

A quibus autem hic tumultus motus fuerat, monachi caute omittunt. In hoc tumultu Edgarus regis frater regni partem obtinet. Hi multis utrinque illatis praeliis, regni vires labefactarunt: sed Edgarus tandem potior, convocato ad Brandan fordiam regni concilio, fratris Edwini acta et decreta rescindit, ablatas ecclesiis et monasteriis opes restituit, Dunstanumque ab exsilio ad pristinum honorem revocat, deinde ad episcopatum Wigornensem, nolentem, ut aiunt, et volentem promovit, postea ad Londinensem, tandem biennio vix transacto ad Cantuariensem archipraesulatum.

Privilegium quo rex Edgarus confirmat Dorobernensem Ecclesiam matrem esse et dominam aliarum Ecclesiarum regni sui.

(Datum anno 959, sed hic occasione superioris concilii collocatum.)

Anno Dominicae incarnationis 958 [cor. 950]. Ego nempe Edgarus rex Anglorum, divinaque concedente clementia monarchus, regum antiquorum Ethelberti et successorum illius, ac archiepiscoporum Brythwaldi et Athelardi statuta, et privilegia monasteriorum Kancegenum, cum venerabilis archipontificis Dunstani consultu atque consilio, ad maledictionem impiorum raptorum, imo magis Deo favente ad benevolentiam justorumque benedictionem, aeterna conclusione renovamus, et in Domino summo roboramus, statuentes,

Ut Ecclesia Christi in Dorobernia aliarum Ecclesiarum regni nostri mater sit et domina, et cum suis omnibus perpetualiter sit ubique libera, praeter expeditionem, pontis et arcis constructionem.

Charta concessa novo monasterio Wintoniae

Incipit charta privilegii Edgari benignissimi principis concessa novo monasterio Wintonio quod modo Hyda appellatur; cujus rubrica sic cancellatur:

EDGAR rex hoc privilegium novo edidit monasterio, de omnipotenti Domino ejusque genitrici Mariae eju laudis magnalia concessit.

Omnipotens, totius machinae conditor, ineffabili pietate universa mirifice moderatur quae condidit, qui coaeterno videlicet Verbo, quaedam ex nihilo edidit, quaedam ex informi subtilis artifex propagavit materia. Angelica quippe creatura, ut informis materia, nullis rebus existentibus, divinitus formata luculento resplenduit vultu. Male, proh dolor! libero utens arbitrio, contumaci arrogans fastu, Creatori universitatis famulari dedignans, semetipsum Creatori aequiparans, aeterni barathri incendiis cum suis complicibus demersus, jugi merito cruciatur miseria. Hoc itaque themate totius sceleris peccatum exorsum est.

II. Quare hominem condidit, et quid ei commisit.

Evacuata animaque [forte, namque HARD.] polorum sede, et eliminata tumidi fastus spurcitia, summus totius bonitatis Arbiter lucidas coelorum sedes non sine cultore passus torpere, formatis ex informi materia diversarum rerum speciebus, hominem tandem ex limo conditum, vitae spiraculo ad sui formavit similitudinem, cui universa totius cosmi superficie condita subjiciens, seipsum suosque posteros sibi subjecit, quatenus ejus exsecutura posteritas angelorum suppleret numerum, coelorum sedibus superbia turgente detrusum.

III. Qualiter in paradiso sine crimine conversatus sit.

Qui paradisiacae voluptatis amoenitate locatus, nullius rei patiebatur dispendium, sed ei totius mundi ad votum suppeditabat facultas. Totius namque bonitatis ubertate frueni nulla ei res instita resistebat. Amore Altithrono devote obsequenti creatura cuncta famulabatur subjecta. Fruebatur laetabundus Creatoris tripudio, et angelorum alacriter utebatur consortio. Non eum corporalis debilitabat imbecillitas, nec animi affligebat anxietas. Non typho levis raptabatur superbiae, sed suo se conjungens auctori, humilis pollebat mirifice. Non eum inanis tumidum vexabat gloria, sed devotum Creatoris magnificabat memoria. Non invidia eum alieno torquebat profectu, sed charitas jugiter laetabatur amplexu. Non ira cruciabatur infestus, sed charitatis tranquillitate leviabatur patientissimus. Non eum tristitia moerore dejiciebat, sed gaudii spiritalis spe pollente florebat. Non avaritia nimium incitabatur cupidus, sed dapsilitatis studio exercebatur largissimus. Non illicito massicus delectabatur edulio, sed parcitate contentus licito utebatur cibario. Non luxuria eum stimulabat nefaria, sed continentia competens constringebat ad praemia; omnium polycrates virtutum, cunctis carens adversis, omnibus florens prosperis, rite pollebat ingenuus.

IV. Quomodo coelum sine morte conscendere confidebat, et diabolus invidus ne ascenderet impediebat.

Qui prole ad numerum patrata, superbientium angelorum universa comitante prosapia, fine loto [forte, sine loco., HARD.] gustato ligni vetiti fructu, aethereos aeternae beatitudinis suggestus triniatim cum Domino regnans conscendere macrobius confidebat. Invidus igitur hoc animadvertens Zabulus, nimia perculsus invidia, rimari callide versutus coeperat, qui insidiis, ne ad tantam numinis conscenderet gloriam, subdolus deciperet; pro nihilo forte ducens concessa, illicita nimium allubescendo laudans, mulierem admodum fragilem pellexit. Quae sui detrimenti minime contenta, virum muliebriter victum blandis suasionibus delinitum, exili, heumalo gustato sibi similem faciens, perdidit.

V. Quomodo in hac miseria omnibus privati virtutibus dejiciuntur, tandemque cataclysmate de [...] [lege dempti., HARD.].

Utrique tandem praefatis privati odonariis, paradisi eliminati metis, in praesentis vitae aerumna miserrimi dejiciuntur, contemnentes conditorem, a cunctis insequuntur creatis. Vita desiit, mors inolevit. Virtutum caterva recedente, vitiorum cumulus successit. Succedente nepotum prosapia, successit cumulata criminum collegio (collectio): universi cum suis sceleribus cataclysmate dempti, tandem, octo utriusque sexus reservatis, tabescendo deficiunt. Vitiis copiose surgentibus, Conditor se hominem fecisse indoluit. Postremo misericors mortalibus, ut pollicitus est, succurrit.

VI. Quomodo Christus natus sua nos passione redemit, et coelos conscendere fecit.

Stella emicuit matutina, quae suo radio mundi tenebras fugaret. Fausta resplenduit Maria, cujus utero virginali Christus ineffabiliter editus, peccatorum tenebras mediator clementissimus dempsit. Viguit Christus virtutibus plenus. Incanduit Judaea ingenti rancore repleta. Carnem suscipiens pro nobis pati voluit; quod ejus permissu infelix audacter complevit Judaea. Ligno quippe perditum, ligni scandens gabulum, genus redemit humanum. Universas namque hominum daemon nationes ludificando insultans, jure ut mandati transgressorem possidens, morte multabat perpetua. Sanguis vero a mortuis ultorem trophaeo crucis divisit. Praedam de perfidi leonis ore tulit, secumque super aethera vehens superius angelorum coetibus consociavit, ut cum eo communi contubernio fruentes, bonitate perspicui, virtutum omnium ubertate referti, expertes peccati, omni contagione privati, sine fine post diem judicii restauratis corporibus exsultantes regnarent. Hanc praecipuam sine dubio gloriam credentibus, qui Trinitatis veraeque unitatis fidem bonis insudantes operibus sectantur, pollicitus, non credentibus supplicium minatus aeternum perpetuis barathri incendiis, justissime spopondit.

VII. De benevolo regis meditamine.

Hinc ego Edgarus, divina favente gratia totius Albionis basileus, rimari magnopere coeperam quid operum studio exercerem, ut ad tantam gloriam perveniens, Christi sanctorumque ejus coelo collocatorum contubernio coronatus fruerer, tantamque inferni miseriam divitarem. Instigante etenim Domini clementia, occurrit animo ut ipse criminibus cessarem cunctis, atque bonis operibus insistens, forma factus gregi, quousque nostri regiminis gubernamine degentes lucrifacerem. Quosdam igitur suasionibus invitans ad praemia, quosdam terroribus compellens ad gloriam, bona aedificans, mala, ut Domino faciente potui, dissipavi. Scriptum quippe per Jeremiam memini prophetam: Ecce constitui te super gentes et super regna, ut evellas, et destruas, et disperdas, et dissipes, et aedifices, et plantes (Jerem. I). Talibus igitur exhortatus doctoribus, quibus nos Dominus per prophetam clementer admonuit, agens Christo favente in terris quod ipse juste egit in coelis, extricans videlicet Domini cultura criminum spurcitias, virtutum semina sedulus agricola inserui.

VIII. Qua ratione clericos eliminans, monachos collocavit.

Timens ne aeternam incurrerem miseriam, si adepta potestate non facerem quod ipse, qui operatur omnia quae in coelo vult et in terra, suis exemplis justus examinator innotuit, vitiosorum cuneos canonicorum e diversis nostri regiminis coenobiis Christi vicarius eliminavi; quod nullis mihi intercessionibus prodesse poterant, sed potius, ut beatus ait Gregorius, justi vindictam Judicis provocarent, qui vicariis vitiorum naevis contaminati, non agentes quae Deus jubendo volebat, omnia quae nolebat rebelles faciebant; avidus inquisitor advertens gratos Domino monachorum cuneos, qui pro nobis incunctanter intercederent, nostri juris monasteriis devotus hilariter collocavi.

IX. Quod sancti Spiritus gratia compunctus abbatem et monachos in novo constituit monasterio.

Hac itaque ratione, sancti Spiritus attactus flamine, locum Domini mundans Wintoniensis ecclesiae, novi monasterii arcisterium [forte, asceterium. HARD. hoc est, monasterium] nostro salvatori ejusque genitrici semper virgini Mariae, et omnibus apostolicis, cum caeteris sanctis, dicatum restauravi. Sciens scriptum: Consentientes et facientes pari constringuntur poena rebellionis, Omnipotentis voluntati obviantes. Possessionem Domini usurpare non sustinens, clericos lascivientes repuli, ac veros Dei cultores monachico gradu fungentes, qui pro nostris nostrorumque inibi quiescentium excessibus sedulo intercederent servitio, quo eorum intercessionibus nostri regiminis status vigeret munitus, abbatem Christo cooperante eligens, Altithrono subjectus illic devote ordinavi. Hoc subnixe efflagitans deposco, ut quod in suis egi, hoc agat in mihi ab ipso collatis, scilicet adversarios nostros dejiciens, amicos sublimando provehat, ut inimicos sanctae Dei Ecclesiae deprimens, amicos ejus monachos videlicet beatificans justificavi.

X. De illorum anathemate qui monachis insidiantur.

Si autem qualibet occasione, diabolo instigante, contigerit, ut fastu superbientis arrogantiae, dejecti canonici, monachorum gregem, quem ego venerans cum pastore in Dei constitui possessione, dejicere insidiando voluerint, agatur de eis et de omnibus qui quolibet munere caecati juvamen eis impenderint, quod actum est de angelis superbientibus, et de protoplasto diaboli fraude seducto, ut paradisi videlicet limitibus [forte, liminibus. HARD.] sublimibusque coelorum sedilibus ejecti, cum iis qui Domini famulatum aspernantes contempserunt, barathri incendiis detrusi, jugi crucientur miseria. Nec inde evulsi se glorientur evasisse tormenta, sed cum Juda Christi proditore ejusque complicibus, Acheronte conglutinati, frigore stridentes, fervore perusti, laetitia privati, moerore anxii, catenis igneis compediti, lictorum metu perculsi, scelerum memoria confusi, totius bonitatis recordatione semoti, aeterno lugubres puniantur cruciatu.

XI. Item de anathemate insidiantium.

Qui autem jam praedictos novi Wintoniensis ecclesiae coenobii monachos, vel quoslibet ejusdem ordinis nostro regimine degentes, monasteriis, quae vitiorum spurcitiis expurgans, Jesu Christo Domino nostro, victo daemone, acquisivi, eliminare praesumens voluerit, anathema sit; et eadem maledictione qua Cain parricida, qui fratrem suum Abel, stimulante invidia, lividus interemit mastigia, adductus est, sine termino teneatur obnoxius; atque in Dei persecutione continuo perseverans, in hac vita nullum dignitatis acquirat honorem, nec in futuro sine miseria nunquam persistat, sed cum Anania et Saphira una Styx porragine [forte voragine] ejulantem crucians complectatur.

XII. De benedictione monachos venerantium.

Quicunque praetitulatos monachos bonis quibuslibet locupletans ditare voluerit, Creator cunctitenens clementer eos eorumque progeniem totius ubertate prosperitatis hic et in futuro saeculo ditando locupletet. Scriptis decenter eorum in libro vitae nominibus, cum Christo portionem in coelorum habitaculis habeant, qui monachos suos, quos nostris congregatos temporibus possidet, vel verbis, vel factis, sanctitatis studio honoraverint.

XIII. Quales et qualiter monachi in hoc monasterio conserventur.

Regulares igitur monachi, non saeculares, in praefato, Christo comite, degentes monasterio, regulae moribus obtemperent, Patres venerantes spirituales, sanctorum Patrum imitentur exempla, nil agentes, nisi quod communis monasterii regula, vel majorum demonstravit norma. A saecularibus igitur pompis remoti, toto nisu corporis custodiant et animae castitatem. Humilitatis studio pollentes, et corpus parcimoniae vigore minuentes, alacri constringant animo. Civium convivae intra urbem perpetuo interdictu fieri erubescant. In civitate degentes, in refectorio pompaticas lascivasque saecularium delicias ut melancholiam aporiantes, licitis charitatum utantur cibariis; extra refectorium autem minime, nisi in domo infirmorum aegroti decubuerint, edentes licite quae jussi fuerint. Sacri summique ordinis hospites, si ratio exegerit, et peregrini ordinati, longo terrarum spatio venientes, ad abbatis mensam in refectorio cautissime invitentur; laicis in hospitio condecens exhibeatur humanitas. Monachorum quispiam manducandi vel bibendi cum eis secundum Patrum decreta licentiam non habeat; in refectorio autem edendi causa vel bibendi non introducantur, Pauperes, ut Christi, ingenti cordis suscipiantur tripudio.

XIV. De abbatum electione.

Divinarum studio Scripturarum luculentissime eruditi, orationum frequentia assidue occupati, charitatis amplexu laetissimi, fidei exercitio promptissimi, spe provehente sincerissimi, pace concorditer fixi, omniumque virtutum flore decorati, ad finem usque, coeptum tantae bonitatis initium, Christo juvante, perducentes, eadem gloriosi fruantur libertate, quam beatus patronus Benedictus omnibus regulae praecepto subjectis instituit, scilicet ut post abbatis obitum tunc temporis regentis, abbatem. [...] ordinent congregatione, quem sibi omnis concors congregatio, sive pars quamvis minima congregationis, salubriori clegerit consilio.

XV. Qualiter rex abbatem et monachos venerans muniat.

Reges itaque, quicunque nostri fuerint successores, nullam extraneam personam jus tyrannidis super monachos exercentem imponant, ne forte Deus eos damnans, et regno deponat et vita. Electum vero a fratribus Christi vicarium dignanter suscipiant, eumque charitatis igne succensi locupletando venerentur; juvamen, inquantum indiguerit, Christi amore compuncti, alacriter impendant. Mutuo namque confortati juvamine, in nullo a regulae praeceptis discordantes, Domini gregem, non mercenarii, sed pastores fidissimi, luporum rictibus eximentes, intrepidi defendant.

XVI. Qualiter abbas et monachi regem a daemonum tentatione eripiant.

Abbas autem armis succinctus spiritualibus, monachorum cuneo hinc inde vallatus, charismatum coelestium rore perfusus, aereas daemonum expugnans versutias, regem, omnemque sui regiminis clerum, Christo, cujus virtute dimicant, juvante, a rabida hostium persecutione invisibilium solerter spiritus gladia defendens, fidei scuto subtili protegens tutamine, robusto praelians triumpho, miles eripiat imperterritus.

XVII. Qualiter rex abbatem et monachos ab hominum persecutione defendat.

Rex itidem terrenus, coelestis castra regis fortissimo roborans munimine, armis saecularibus visibiles expugnans adversarios, hostiumque rabiem saevientium annihilando dejiciens, Conditoris sui pascua gregemque sollicita inexpugnabilis tueatur custodia, quatenus ad vitae bravium perveniens, aeternis tripudians fruatur bonis, quae nec oculus videre aliquatenus potuit humanus, nec in hominis cor ullatenus ascendit quae praeparavit Deus diligentibus se.

XVIII. De monasticae possessionis libertate.

Sint praefati monasterii rura, omnis monachorum possessio, in rebus magnis vel modicis, internis vel externis, in urbanis vel suburbanis, praediis, campis, pratis, pascuis, silvis, molendinis, rivulorum cursibus, aeterna libertate in Christi nomine ejusque Genitricis ditata.

XIX. Quod nullus saecularium monasterii possessionem illicite usurpet.

Saecularium quispiam ausu temerario jus tyrannidis non in Christi cultura praesumptuosus exerceat; non minuet, instigante diabolo, quod sancti Spiritus instinctu tam a me quam a praedecessoribus meis, necnon a catholicis utriusque sexus hominibus, largiflua concessum est dapsilitate.

XX. De benedictione augentium.

Augenti tribuat rerum cunctarum Opifex tranquillum vitae praesentis excursum, longaevum instantis temporis, futurum aeternae beatitudinis talionem, sufficientem victualium ubertatem, interminabile prosperitatis augmentum, copiosum virtutum omnium juvamen.

XXI. De maledictione minuentium.

Minuentem perpetua possideat miseria; in Domini manens persecutione, ejus Genitricis sanctorumque omnium incurrat offensam; praesentis vitae adversitas illi semper eveniat; nulla eis bonitatis accidat prosperitas; omnia ejus peculia inimici astantes diripiant; in futuro autem, aeterni miserrimum cum haedis in sinistra positum damnent cruciatus, si non satisfactione emendaverit congrua quod in Domini usurpans detraxit censura.

XXII. Quibus modis saecularibus obtemperent, et quod nullus reatus hoc Domini privilegium minuere valeat.

Tribus tantummodo causis, saecularibus obtemperent praeceptis, rata videlicet expeditione, pontis, arcisve constructione; alias aeterna ditati glorientur libertate. Reatus quidpiam si, incitante daemone, seductus, vel abbas, vel fratrum aliquis fragiliter, quod absit, contraxerit, justitia purgante secundum regulae praeceptum abolitus damnetur, maneatque praefatae munificentiae libertas Altithrono per nostram humilitatem oblata, ad monachorum usus gratuite sibi famulantium inviolabilis, aeterna libertate jucunda, quia Deus, qui hanc privilegii largifluam donationem, locumque cum universa monachorum familia, juraque omnia sacro subjecta coenobio possidet, nunquam reatum commisit, nec ullo unquam tempore committet. Sit igitur praefata libertas aeterna, quia Deus libertatis possessor aeternus est.

XXIII. Quoties et quare in anni circulo hoc fratribus legatur privilegium.

Anno incarnationis Dominicae nongentesimo sexagesimo sexto scripta est hujus privilegii syngrapha, his testibus consentientibus, quorum inferius nomina ordinatim charaxantur.

SUBSCRIPTIONES.

  Ego Edgar, divina largiente gratia, Anglorum basileus, hoc privilegii donum nostro largiens Redemptori, locoque ejus sanctissimo, primus omnium regum, monachorum inibi collegium constituens, manu propria signum hagiae crucis imprimens confirmavi.
  Ego Dunstan, Dorobernensis Ecclesiae archiepiscopus, largifluam benevoli regis donationem venerans, crucis signaculo corroboravi.
  Ego Eadmund, clytos legitimus praefati filius, crucis signaculum, infantuli florens aetate, propria indidi manu.
  Ego Edward, eodem rege clyto procreatus, praefatam patris munificentiam crucis signo consolidavi.
  Ego Aelfthryth, legitima praefati regis conjux, mea legatione monachos eodem loco rege annuente constituens, crucem impressi.
  Ego Eadgifa, praedicti regis ava, hoc opus egregium crucis thaumate consolidavi.
  Ego Oscytyl, Eboracensis Ecclesiae archiepiscopus, firmavi.
  Ego Athelwold, Ecclesiae Wintoniensis episcopus, regis gloriosissimi benevolentiam, abbatem mea altum mediocritate, et alumnos quos educavi, illi commendans, crucis signaculo benedixi.
  Ego Aelfstan, Londoniensis Ecclesiae pontifex, consolidavi.
  Ego Osulf, episcopus, confirmavi.
  Ego Oswold, episcopus, consignavi.
  Ego Bysentelm, episcopus, confirmavi.
  Eaelfstan, episcopus, consolidavi.

Ego Eadelm, episcopus, confirmavi.
Ego Athulf, episcopus, consignavi.
Ego Urynryge, episcopus, confirmavi.
Aercwig, abbas, consolidavi.
Ego Osgar, abbas, consignavi.
Ego Orobyrihe, abbas.
Ego Aelfstan, abbas.
Ego Adelgar, abbas primus huic loco abbas ordinatus.
Ego Osdgar, dux.
Ego Aethelstan, dux.
Ego Athelwine, dux.
Ego Aethelweard, m.
Ego Elfweard, m.
Ego Wulrtan, m.

Omnes qui nominatim huic privilegio regis jussu descripti videntur, posteritatis nostrae prosapiam subnixe deposcimus, ut manuum nostrarum vadimonium Christi cruce firmatum nequaquam violantes irritum faciant; si successorum quispiam humilitatis ausu violare praesumpserit, corporis et sanguinis Jesu Christi participatione privatus, perpetua damnatus perditione, anathema sit, nisi divino propitiante respectu ad huminem satisfactionem resipiscens conversus fuerit.

ALIA CHARTA EDGARI REGIS, Qua nullos unquam fuisse perhibet in Wintoniensi hoc coenobio monachos, ante hos quos ipse jam introduxit e monasterio Abingioniensi.

Annuente Altithroni moderatoris imperio totius Albionis triniatim potitus regimine, non immemor ob hoc recidiva fore concessa, ut his strenue aeterna lucrarer; quapropter ego Edgar, totius Britanniae basileus, quasdam villas, ut nominantur, Dunkitone habens, quinque hydas terrae, et ecclesiam Sueyse, cum viginti octo hydis terrae, et ecclesiam Titlescumbe cum decem hydis terrae, et quamdam ruris portionem, duos videlicet cassatos terrae, loco qui celebri Wynterburna nuncupatur vocabulo, do et concedo in puram et perpetuam eleemosynam novae Wintoniensi ecclesiae, B. Petro apostolorum principi dicatae, necnon S. Edotio, cujus reliquiae inibi miraculis clarescunt, cum omnibus utensilibus, pratis videlicet, pascuis, rivulis, aeterna largita sint haereditate perspicuis, ut canonicos qui incorrigibiles perdurarent de ecclesia dicta ejeci, monachos de Abundonie loco substitui. Sint autem praedictae villae, rus, mansiones, terrae, rivuli, omni terrenae servitutis jugo liberae in perpetuum, tribus exceptis, rata videlicet expeditione, pontis, arcisve restauratione. Si quis autem hanc nostram donationem in aliud quam constituimus transferre voluerit, privatus consortio sanctae Dei Ecclesiae, aeternis barathri incendiis lugubris jugiter cum Juda Christi proditore ejusque complicibus puniatur, si non satisfactione emendaverit congrua quod contra nostrum deliquit decretum.

Leges ecclesiasticae

TITULI CAPITULORUM.
I. De immunitate Ecclesiae, et debitis eidem reddendis.
II. De censu ecclesiastico, sive primitiis seminum.
III. De decimis.
IV. De denario in domos singulas imposito.
V. De diebus festis, et jejunio.

LEGES EDGARI REGIS.
Leges, quas Edgarus rex frequenti senatu ad Dei gloriam, regiae majestatis ornamentum ac reipublicae utilitatem sancivit:

I. Primum, ecclesia Dei jura atque immunitates suas omnes habeto; decimas quisque primariae (cui is fuerit subjectus) ecclesiae, ut ipsum quidem circumducitur aratrum, dato, sive id in praediis thanorum propriis, sive in terris villicorum fuerit.

II. Thanus si in terra ex scripto possessa templum habuerit, circum quod fuerit destinatus sepulturae locus, decimarum suarum trientem unum in id conferre ei integrum esto. Sin circa templum nullus fuerit designatus humationi locus, dato qui est fundi dominus sacerdoti novem partium reliquiarum quantulum visum fuerit. Atque ex omni quidem ingenuorum terra, ipsae seminum primitiae, primariae penduntor ecclesiae.

III. Quisque fetuum decimas omnes ante Pentecosten persolvito; terrae quidem fructuum decimas ante Aequinoctium pendito; ipsas autem seminum primitias sub festum divi Martini reddito. Si quis non solverit, poenas, ut judiciali libro proditum est, dato. Atque si quis decimas, ad eum quem diximus modum, dare noluerit, praepositus regius, illius loci episcopus, et sacerdos conveniunto, atque eo vel invito decimam ecclesiae, cui debeatur, partem, nona ei reliqua facta, reddunto. Quod ad residuas octo partes attinet, quatuor dominus, quatuor episcopus habeto; id quod fiat, sive is fuerit minister regis, sive thani alterius cujuscunque.

IV. Denarius autem in domos singulas impositus, ante festum divi Petri redditor. Qui tum non solverit, denarium illum ac alios praeterea triginta ad Romam comportato, certaque litterarum testificatione, domum rediens, se eo detulisse confirmato, ac regi denique centum viginti solidos numerato. Si quis secundo non dederit, denarium illum ac praeterea ter denos Romam deferat, regique postquam redierit ducentos solidos dependito. Sin tertio deliquerit, rebus suis omnibus exuitor.

V. Dies Sabbati ab ipsa diei Saturni hora pomeridiana tertia usque in lunaris diei difuculum festus agitor; qui non celebrarit, poenas in judiciali libro descriptas pendito. Caeteri autem dies perinde ut fuerint a sacerdote indicti, festi aguntor. Instituta etiam quam religiosissime observantor jejunia.

LEGUM ECCLESIASTICARUM EDGARI REGIS PRISCA VERSIO.
I. De debitis Ecclesiae reddendis.
II. De ecclesiis ubi est coemeterium.
III. De terminis decimandis.
IV. De nolente decimas dare.
V. De non solventibus denarium S. Petri.
VI. De solemnitatibus et terminis observandis.

Hoc est institutum quod Edgarus rex consilio sapientum suorum instituit Deo ad gloriam, et sibi ad regiam dignitatem, et genti suae ad commodum.

I. Primum est, ut ecclesiae Dei recti sui dignae sint, et reddatur omnis decimatio ad matrem ecclesiam cui parochia adjacet de terra thaynorum et villanorum, sicut aratrum peragrabit.

II. Si quis thaynorum sit qui feodo suo ecclesiam habeat ubi coemeterium sit, det ei tertiam partem decimae suae. Si non sit ibi atrium, det ex suis novem partibus presbytero quod vult, et etiam omne ciricsceatum ad matrem ecclesiam de omni libera domo.

III. Et omnis decimatio juventutis reddita sit ad Pentecosten, et terrae frugum ad Aequinoctium, et omne ciricsceatum ad festum S. Martini, per plenam forisfacturam quam judicialis liber dicit.

IV. Si quis decimam dare noluerit, sicut diximus, adest praepositus regis et episcopi sacerdos [f. et episcopus, et sacerdos, etc.] illius ecclesiae, et reddat ecclesiae cui pertinebit decimam suam, et nonam partem dimittant ei qui decimam suam detinuit, et octo partes in duo dividantur, dimidium domino, dimidium episcopo, sit homo regis, sit homo thayni.

V. Et omnis heordpen reddat ad festum S. Petri: et qui non solvit ad terminum illum, deferat eum Romam, et etiam triginta denarios, et afferat inde significationem quod tantum ibi reddidit. Et cum redierit domum, emendet centum viginti solidos. Et si iterum reddere nolit, deferat cum Romam, et emendationem eamdem. Et cum redierit, emendet centum viginti solidos regi. Ad tertiam vicem, si adhuc non reddiderit, perdat totum quod habebit.

VI. Et solemne diei Dominicae conservetur ab bora nona Sabbati usque ad lucidum diei Lunae, superforisfactura quam liber judiciorum dicit et docet. Et alia festivitas, sicut a sacerdote nuntiabitur. Et omne indictum jejunium cum omni devotione servetur.

LAWS & CHARTERS

Oratio ad Dunstanum Oswaldum et Ethelwaldum

Quoniam magnificavit misericordiam suam Dominus facere nobiscum, dignum est, o Patres reverendissimi, ut innumeris illius beneficiis, dignis respondeamus operibus. Neque enim in gladio nostro possidemus terram, et brachium nostrum non servavit nos, sed dextra ejus, et brachium sanctum ejus, quoniam complacuit illi in nobis. Justum proinde est, ut qui omnia subjecit sub pedibus nostris, subjiciamus illi et nos et animas nostras, et, ut hi, quos nobis subdidit, ejus subdantur legibus, non segniter elaboremus. Et mea quidem interest laicos cum aequitatis jure tractare, inter virum et proximum suum justum judicium facere, punire sacrilegos, rebelles comprimere, eripere inopem de manu fortiorum ejus, egenum et pauperem a diripientibus eum. Sed et meae sollicitudinis est, ecclesiarum ministris, gregibus monachorum, choris virginum et necessaria eorum procurare, ac saluti, et quieti, vel paci consulere. De quorum omnium moribus ad nos [f., ad vos] spectat examen, si vixerint continenter, si honeste se habeant ad eos qui foris sunt; si divinis officiis solliciti, si ad docendum populum assidui, si victu sobrii, si habitu moderati, si in judiciis sint discreti. Pace vestra loquor, reverendi Patres, si ista solerti scrutinio curassetis, non tam horrenda et abominanda ad aures nostras de clericis pervenissent.

Taceo quod non est illis corona patens, nec tonsura conveniens; at in veste lascivia, insolentia in gestu, in verbis turpitudo, interioris hominis produnt insaniam. Praeterea in divinis officiis quanta sit negligentia, cum sacris vigiliis vix interesse dignentur, cum ad sacra missarum solemnia ad ludendum, subridendum magis quam ad psallendum, congregari videantur. Dicam quod boni lugent, mali rident; dicam dolens (et si tamen dici potest) quomodo diffluant in comessationibus, in ebrietatibus, in cubilibus et impudicitiis, ut jam domus clericorum putentur postribula meretricum, conciliabulum histrionum. Ibi aleae, ibi saltus et cantus; ibi usque ad medium noctis spatium protractae in clamore et horrore vigiliae. Sic patrimonia regum, eleemosynae pauperum, imo, quod magis est, illius pretiosi sanguinis pretium profligatur. Ad hoc ergo exhauserunt Patres nostri thesauros suos? ad hoc fiscus regius, detractis redditibus multis, elargitus est? ad hoc ecclesiis Christi agros et possessiones regalis munificentia contulit, ut deliciis clericorum meretrices ornentur, luxuriosa convivia praeparentur, canes, ac aves, et talia ludicra comparentur? Hoc milites clamant, plebs submurmurat, mimi cantant et saltant, et vos negligitis, vos parcitis, vos dissimulatis! Ubi gladius Levi et zelus Simeonis, qui ut scorto abutentes filia Jacob, Sichimitas (eorum habentes figuram qui Christi ecclesiam pollutis actibus foedant) etiam circumcisos succiderunt? Ubi spiritus Moysis, qui caput vituli adorantibus etiam domesticis sui sanguinis non pepercit? Ubi pugio Phinees sacerdotis, qui fornicantem cum Madianita confodiens, sancta hac aemulatione Deum placavit iratum? Ubi spiritus Petri, cujus virtute perimitur avaritia, haeresis Simoniaca condemnatur?

Aemulamini, o sacerdotes, aemulamini vias Domini, et jusiitias Dei nostri. Tempus insurgendi contra eos qui dissiparunt egem Dei. Ego Constantini, vos Petri, gladium habetis in manibus. Jungamus dexteras, gladium gladio copulemus, ut ejiciantur extra castra leprosi, ut purgetur sanctuarium Domini, et ministrent in templo filii Levi, qui dixit patri et matri: Nescio vos, et fratribus suis: Ignoro vos. Agite, quaeso, sollicite, ne poeniteat nos fecisse quod fecimus, dedisse quod dedimus; si viderimus illud non in Dei obsequium, sed in pessimorum luxuriam impunita libertate consumi. Moveant vos sanctorum reliquiae, in quibus insultant; veneranda altaria, ante quae insaniunt. Moveat vos antecessorum nostrorum mira devotio, quorum eleemosynis vesania clericalis abutitur. Proavus meus Edwardus, ut scitis, omnem terram suam ecclesiis et monasteriis decimavit. Sanctae memoriae atavus meus Aluredus, ut ecclesiam ditaret, non patrimonio, non sumptibus, non redditibus parcendum putavit. Avus meus senior Edwardus quanta contulerit ecclesiis, paternitatem vestram non latet. Pater meus, et frater, quibus donariis Christi altaria cumulaverint, meminisse vos decet.

O Pater Patrum, Dunstane, contemplare, quaeso, Patris mei oculos ab illa lucida coeli plaga in te radiantes. Audi querulas ejus voces cum quadam pietate in tuis auribus resonantes: Tu mihi, Pater Dunstane, tu mihi de construendis monasteriis, de ecclesiis aedificandis, consilium salubre dedisti: tu mihi adjutor in omnibus et cooperator exstitisti: te quasi pastorem, patrem, et episcopum animae meae, morumque meorum custodem elegi. Quando tibi non parui? Quos unquam thesauros tuis consiliis praetuli? Quas possessiones, te praecipiente, non sprevi? Si quid pauperibus erogandum existimabas, praesto fui. Si quid conferendum ecclesiis judicabas, non distuli. Si quid monachis clericisve deesse querebaris, supplevi. Aeternam dicebas eleemosynam esse, nec aliam fructuosiorem, quam quod monasteriis ecclesiisve confertur, quo Dei servi sustententur, et quod superest, pauperibus erogetur. O pretiosam eleemosynam, et dignum animae pretium! O peccatis nostris salubre remedium! quod a sinu Sibyllae in peregrini muris pellicula foetet, quod ejus auriculas ornat, quod componit digitulos, quod corpus delicatum in bysso stringit et purpura. Ecce, Pater, eleemosynarum fructus mearum, et tuae permissionis effectus.

Quid huic querimoniae respondebis? Scio, scio: Cum videbas furem, non currebas cum eo, nec cum adulteris portionem tuam ponebas. Arguisti, obsecrasti atque increpasti. Contempta verba sunt, veniendum est ad verbera, et non deerit tibi potestas regia. Habes hic tecum venerabilem Patrem Ethelwaldum Wintoniensem episcopum; habes reverendum praesulem Wigorniensem Oswaldum; vobis istud committo negotium, ut et episcopali censura, et regia auctoritate, turpiter viventes de ecclesiis ejiciantur, et ordinate viventes introducantur.

Charta Malmesburiensis

Ego Edgarus, totius Albionis basileus, necnon maritimorum seu insulanorum regum circumhabitantium, adeo ut nullius progenitorum meorum subjectione, largiflua Dei gratia suppetente, sublimatus, quid imperii mei potissimum Regi regum dono darem, tanti memor honoris, solertius saepe tractavi. Piae igitur fautrix devotionis pervigili meae studiositati superna subito insinuavit pietas, quaeque in regno meo sancta restaurare monasteria, quae velut muscivis scindulis, cariosisque tabulis, tigno tenus visibiliter diruta, sic (quod majus est) intus a servitio Dei ferme vacue fuerant neglecta. Idiotis nempe clericis ejectis, nullis regularis religionis disciplinae subjectis, plurimis in locis sanctioris seriei, scilicet monachici habitus, praefeci pastores, ad ruinosa quaeque templorum redintegranda opulentos eis fiscalium munerum exhibens sumptus. Quorum unum, nomine Eluricum, virum in omnibus ecclesiasticum, famosissimi constitui custodem coenobii, quod Angli bifario vocitant onomate Maldemelsburh. Cui pro commoditate animae meae, ob Salvatoris nostri, ejusque Θεότοκου semper virginis Mariae, necnon apostolorum Petri et Pauli, Aldelmique almi praesulis, honorem, particulam terrae, et nominatim terram cum pratis et silvis, munifica liberalitate restitui. Haec a praedictis accommodata clericis a contentioso injuste possessa est Edolnoto: sed superstitiosa subtilique ejus disceptatione a sapientibus meis audita, et conflictatione illius mendosa ab eisdem me praesente convicta, monasteriali a me reddita est usui, anno Dominicae incarnationis nongentesimo septuagesimo quarto, regno vero mei decimo quarto, regiae conversationis primo. Haec Malmesburiensis.

SUBSCRIPTIONES.

Ego Edgarus, totius Albionis finitimorumque regum basileus, cum signo sanctae crucis istud chirographum confirmavi.

Ego Dunstanus, Dorobernensis archiepiscopus, istud donum regium hagiae crucis trophaeo corroboravi.
   Ego Oswaldus, Eboracensis archiepiscopus, subscripsi.
   Ego Athelwoldus, episcopus Wintoniensis, consignavi.
   Ego Lefwinus, Dorcacistrensis episcopus, consensi.
   Ego Alstanus, episcopus Londoniensis, annui.
   Ego Turketulus, abbas Croylandiae, subnotavi.
   Ego Athelgarus, abbas novi monasterii Wintoniae, approbavi.
   Ego Adulphus, abbas Burgensis, collaudavi.
   Ego Alferus dux adfui.
   Ego Athelwinus dux astiti.
   Ego Britholdus dux aspexi.
   Et alii.

The Scriptorium Project is the work of a small group of lay people of various apostolic churches who are interested in the preservation, transmission, and translation of the works of the early and medieval church. Our efforts are to make the works of the church fathers accessible to anyone who might have an interest in Christian antiquities and the theological, philosophical, and moral writings that have become the bedrock of Western Civilization.

To-date, our releases have pulled from the Greek, Syriac, Georgian, Latin, Celtic, Ethiopian, and Coptic traditions of Christianity, and have been pulled from sundry local traditions and languages.

Other Selections from the Early Anglo-Saxon Church Series:

Church Laws by Alfred the Great, King of Anglo-Saxons (May 2006)
Church Laws by Guthram, King of East Anglia (Feb. 2007)
Two Works by St. Dunstan of Canterbury (Jan. 2008)
The Eight Principal Vices by St. Aldheim of Malmesbury (May 2013)
For the Catholic Easter and the Roman Tonsure by Ceolfridus of Wiremouth (June 2013)
Penitential (Poenitentiale) by Theodore of Tarsus (July 2013)
Life of St. Augustine of Canterbury by Goscelin of Saint-Bertin (Aug. 2013)
Laws & Charters by Edgar, King of the English (Mar. 2015)
The English Calendar by St. Bede the Venerable (Nov. 2015)
Letter to King Aethelred by Pope John VII (Dec. 2015)
The Life of the Christian by Fastidius of Britain (Apr. 2017)
Privileges of the Abbot of Cantergury by St. Augustine of Canterbury (Sept. 2017)
A Song of Aethelwolf by Aethelwolf of Lindisfarne (Nov. 2017)
Decrees of Aethelbert by St. Aethelbert, King of Kent (Feb. 2019)
Donations by St. Aethelbert, King of Kent (May 2020)
Life of St. Augustine of Canterbury by Goscelin of Saint-Bertin (Dec. 2020)
Canons of the Council of London by Edgar, King of the English (Dec. 2023)

www.ingramcontent.com/pod-product-compliance
Lightning Source LLC
LaVergne TN
LVHW052005060526
838201LV00059B/3843